OTHER MUSIC QUIZ BOO

The BTS Quiz Book

The Ariana Grande Quiz Book

The Taylor Swift Quiz Book

375 Questions to Test a True Swifty

Published by Beartown Press

This book is unofficial, unauthorised and in no way associated with Taylor Swift or any of her artistic or commercial endeavours. It is purely a fun trivia book designed to test the knowledge of Swifties across the world.

ISBN 9798677636394

For you, you lovely reader.

"To me, Fearless is not the absence of fear. It's not being completely unafraid. To me, Fearless is having fears. Fearless is having doubts. Lots of them. To me, Fearless is living in spite of those things that scare you to death." – T.S.

Contents

Introduction

I don't know about you, but I find Taylor Swift one of the most talented popstars around. I mean, she already had the fans and sales (50m albums, 150m singles) to prove it, but even if she didn't, could you imagine anyone else writing *the last great american dynasty*?

She is already legendary. And that's why this quiz book exists. What you have here is 375 questions about Taylor Swift, split into themed rounds of 15 questions each. Answer sheets are located in the second half of the book.

So, will you secure your reputation as the most knowledge Taylor Swift fan around, or will you leave teardrops on your guitar? It's time to find out!

...Ready for it?

General Knowledge

1. When is Taylor Swift's birthday?

2. What is Taylor Swift's zodiac sign?

3. Before she stopped doing it during the Red Tour, which number would Taylor paint on her hand before every show?

4. What is the name of Taylor's production company?

5. What is the name of the record label Taylor signed with after her contract with her previous label expired in 2018?

6. What are Taylor Swift fans called?

7. What is the name of the record label Taylor Swift recorded her first six studio albums with?

8. Who first discovered Taylor Swift?

9. What color are Taylor Swift's eyes?

10. In which year was Taylor Swift the most Googled female music artist?

11. Who is the redhead Taylor Swift sings about in her song *Fifteen*?

12. What is Taylor's middle name?

13. In which year did Taylor remove her entire song catalog from Spotify?

14. What song did Taylor perform on *The Tonight Show with Jimmy Fallon*, reducing him to an emotional wreck?

15. As revealed on *The Ellen DeGeneres Show* in 2014, what sea creature is Taylor Swift afraid of?

Answers on page 63

Songs

1. In which song does Taylor deliver the line "It feels like a perfect day to dress up like hipsters"?

2. What is Taylor's longest song?

3. What was Taylor Swift's debut single?

4. Which song did Taylor Swift sing on the Global Citizen One World: Together at Home benefit concert last April 18, 2020?

5. Which song features the lyric: "Of all the girls tossing rocks at your window"?

6. What is the lead single from Taylor's third studio album?

7. Which song did Taylor Swift donate all its proceeds to the New York City Department of Education?

8. Which Taylor Swift song referenced Bonnie and Clyde?

9. What is the title of Taylor Swift's first-ever original Christmas song?

10. Which Taylor song taps into themes including US politics, gun violence, and mass shootings?

11. Which Taylor Swift song references the Humpty Dumpty nursery rhyme?

12. Which Taylor Swift song was inspired by the Netflix movie *Someone Great*?

13. Which Taylor Swift song includes themes about the East Asian folk myth "the red thread of fate"?

14. Which song did Taylor write in memory of a four-year-old boy who died of neuroblastoma?

15. Which single did Taylor originally write for a talent show during her freshman year in high school?

Answers on page 64

Early Life

1. What was the first song Taylor learned on the guitar?

2. Which US state is Taylor originally from?

3. During her childhood, what did Taylor's father do for a living?

4. Who is Taylor Swift named after?

5. What is the name of Taylor Swift's younger brother?

6. Who taught Taylor Swift to play guitar?

7. What was the first song Taylor Swift wrote?

8. How old was Taylor Swift when her family moved to Nashville, Tennessee?

9. Are the names of Taylor Swift's parents?

10. What is the name of the high school Taylor attended in Tennessee?

11. What was the occupation of Taylor's maternal grandmother, who inspired her to follow her musical dreams?

12. Who was the home team at the basketball game were a 12-year old Taylor Swift sang the National Anthem?

13. Whose documentary pushed Taylor Swift to move to Nashville and pursue a career in music?

14. What was the name of the cafe where Scott Borchetta discovered Taylor Swift at age 15?

15. What is the first name of Taylor's grandfather, which is also the name of her on-screen lover in the *Wildest Dreams* music video?

Answers on page 65

Albums

1. What is the name of Taylor Swift's seventh album?

2. What album did the song *We Are Never Ever Getting Back Together* belong to?

3. In what album era did Taylor Swift refuse to hold interviews about the album?

4. What was the last album Taylor Swift made under Big Machine Records?

5. What was the *Lover* album almost called?

6. What Taylor Swift album was inspired by the show *Game of Thrones*?

7. Which Taylor Swift album was announced less than 24 hours before its release?

8. Which Taylor Swift album inspired writer/director Jennifer Kaytin Robinson to make the film *Someone Great*?

9. How old was Taylor Swift when she released her self-titled debut album?

10. What album does the song *Sad, Beautiful, Tragic* belong to?

11. Which album did Taylor Swift had her debut as a record producer?

12. What album do the songs *Love Story*, *White Horse*, and *You Belong With Me* belong to?

13. How many singles did the *Speak Now* album have?

14. Which album had the album cover where it shows Taylor Swift's face, wearing lipstick and a hat?

15. Which album did Taylor Swift describe as her "official" pop album?

Answers on page 66

'Taylor Swift' Album

1. Which track was her best-performing song that spent 48 weeks on Billboard Hot 100?

2. Which Tim McGraw song was Taylor referencing on the song *Tim McGraw*?

3. What is the name of Taylor Swift's "boyfriend" in the music video for *Tim McGraw*?

4. Who was the guy Taylor Swift talked about on the song *Teardrops On My Guitar*?

5. What is the name of the lover described as a "redneck heartbreak" in the song *Picture To Burn*?

6. Which song features the lyric: "What a rainy ending given to a perfect day"?

7. What was the final single released from the *Taylor Swift* album?

8. Which song was inspired when Taylor learned that one of her best friends suffered from bulimia?

9. Which song was inspired by the long-lasting marriage of Taylor's neighbors?

10. On the deluxe edition of the *Taylor Swift* album, Taylor Swift included the audio for the first phone conversation with who?

11. Who co-wrote most of the songs from the *Taylor Swift* album?

12. Taylor Swift capitalized specific letters in the lyrics from each song in the album booklet to form a hidden message, on the song *Picture to Burn*. What is the hidden message?

13. Which song was Taylor inspired to write after her boyfriend at the time cheated on her?

14. Which song was released as the fourth single?

15. Which song did Taylor Swift write because she and her boyfriend didn't have a song?

Answers on page 67

'Fearless' Album

1. Which song did Taylor Swift write for a member of the country band which opened several shows for her?

2. Which song from the album charted highest on the Billboard Hot 100?

3. Which song was dedicated to Taylor Swift's mom?

4. What is the first track on the platinum edition of *Fearless*?

5. How many tracks does the standard edition of the album include?

6. Which song was part of Team USA's 2008 Summer Olympics soundtrack?

7. On the song *You Belong with Me*, while Taylor Swift was on the bleachers, what was the role of the other girl?

8. Which actor played Taylor's love interest in the music video for *You Belong With Me*?

9. How long did it take Taylor to write the song *Love Story*?

10. Which song was the lead single from the album?

11. In the *You Belong With Me* music video, what is the phrase written on nerdy Taylor's t-shirt?

12. Which song was written after Taylor Swift overheard a male friend talking to his girlfriend on the phone?

13. Which song almost didn't make the album because it was written for Taylor's third album?

14. Which song does the lyric "This love is difficult, but it's real" belong to?

15. With whom did Taylor collaborate on the song *Breathe*?

Answers on page 68

'Speak Now' Album

1. At what age did Taylor release *Speak Now*?

2. Which *Speak Now* track has these lyrics: "Your little hand's wrapped around my finger and it's so quiet in the world tonight"?

3. Which song was written after Kanye stormed the stage to interrupt Taylor's award acceptance speech?

4. Which song was written when Taylor Swift was 16 years old, even before the release of Tim McGraw?

5. Which song was about Taylor's tendency to run from love ("cause it's all I've ever known…")?

6. Which song was about Taylor Swift's encounter with her ex-boyfriend at the 2010 CMT Awards?

7. In the music video for *Mine*, what was the job of Taylor Swift's boyfriend when they first met?

8. Which song includes the lyric: "I've never heard silence quite this loud"?

9. Taylor capitalized specific letters in the lyrics from each song in the *Speak Now* album booklet to form a hidden word about each track. What was the hidden word for *Back to December*?

10. On the song *Back to December,* in which month did the guy see Taylor Swift cry for the first time?

11. Which song had anti-bullying themes?

12. In the *Mean* music video, who was the child actress applauding in the theater at the end?

13. Which song includes the lyrics "You made a rebel of a careless man's careful daughter"?

14. What is the title of the first song in which Taylor Swift apologized to someone?

15. Taylor Swift revealed that the subject in the song *Dear John* was the same as which other *Speak Now* track?

Answers on page 69

'Red' Album

1. What was the second single released from *Red*?

2. On the standard edition of the *Red* album, out of 16 tracks, how many songs did Taylor write alone?

3. Which song described the joys of being a certain age?

4. In the song *Begin Again*, on which day did Taylor Swift watch "it" begin again in a café?

5. On the deluxe edition of the *Red* album, which song had an acoustic version?

6. Which song was the lead single from *Red*?

7. Which song is about falling in love again after a failed relationship?

8. Which song was about a good girl falling for a bad boy in what turns out to be a toxic relationship?

9. Which artist featured on the song *The Last Time*?

10. In the song *Red*, what color was associated with missing "him"?

11. Which music video did Taylor Swift wear a shirt that says "NOT A LOT GOING ON AT THE MOMENT"?

12. In which song did Taylor Swift use colors as metaphors in its lyrics?

13. What is the longest track on the *Red* album?

14. What color did Taylor Swift dye her hair for the *I Knew You Were Trouble* music video?

15. In the standard edition of the album, what is the last song on *Red*?

Answers on page 70

'1989' Album

1. In the song *Out of the Woods*, how many stitches did Taylor Swift's partner get in the hospital room when he hit the brakes too soon?

2. In the *Out of the Woods* music video, what are the animals chasing Taylor Swift?

3. Which actor played Taylor Swift's love interest in the music video of *Wildest Dreams*?

4. In the *Shake It Off* music video, what was the first and last type of dance shown?

5. How many times was the phrase "shake it off" mentioned in the song *Shake It Off*?

6. Which song includes the lyrics "Got a long list of ex-lovers, they'll tell you I'm insane"?

7. Which model played opposite Taylor Swift on the *Blank Space* music video?

8. Which phrase from the song *Style* did Taylor Swift apply for a trademark on?

9. Which music video was filmed in Serengeti, Tanzania?

10. What is the name of Taylor Swift's character in the *Bad Blood* music video?

11. Who was the celebrity that double-crossed Taylor on the *Bad Blood* music video?

12. Including Kendrick Lamar, how many famous cameos were in the *Bad Blood* music video?

13. Which song was about a betrayal of a close friend?

14. What was the name of Taylor Swift's character on the *Wildest Dreams* music video?

15. Which phrase was shown at the beginning of the *Out of the Woods* music video?

Answers on page 71

'Reputation' Album

1. How many times does Taylor Swift say the word "reputation" in her song *End Game*?

2. Which song was the lead single from *reputation*?

3. What drink is mentioned in the song *Gorgeous*? Be specific…

4. In the *…Ready for It?* music video, which name was written in one of the Chinese signs that coincidentally was the name of the video director and Taylor Swift's boyfriend at that time?

5. Which song has a BloodPop remix?

6. Which song includes the lyrics "The old Taylor can't come to the phone right now. Why? Because she's dead!" belong to?

7. What animal represented the *reputation* album in promo shots leading up to its release?

8. Which was the only song to include featured artists?

9. Which song did Taylor Swift sample to create the hook for *Look What You Made Me Do*?

10. Which *Game of Thrones* character inspired the *Look What You Made Me Do* lyrics "I've got a list of names and yours is in red, underlined"?

11. In the *End Game* music video, Taylor Swift was shown in three cities. Where was she when she was hanging out with Ed Sheeran?

12. Which song includes the lyrics "In the middle of the night in my dreams / I know I'm gonna be with you"?

13. Who is the Taylor reference in the lyric "He can be my jailer, Burton to this Taylor", in the song ...*Ready for It?*

14. In the *End Game* music video, which game does Taylor Swift play on a handheld game console?

15. What is the last track on the *reputation* album?

Answers on page 72

'Lover' Album

1. The daughter of which two actors delivered a voiceover cameo on the song *Gorgeous*?

2. What is the opening track on the *Lover* album?

3. On the album art for *You Need to Calm Down*, Taylor Swift sports a giant back tattoo. Which creatures feature in the tattoo?

4. What is the fifth track on the *Lover* album? *The Archer.*

5. On Taylor Swift's song *Lover*, until which month do they keep the Christmas lights on?

6. Which song was dedicated to her mom's battle with cancer?

7. In the song *The Man*, in which location will Taylor Swift "be just like Leo"?

8. In the *You Need to Calm Down* music video, who was the celebrity dressed as a hamburger?

9. As part of the promotion for the song *ME!*, what creature was painted in a mural in The Gulch neighborhood of Nashville, Tennessee?

10. What is the name of Taylor Swift's male alter ego in the music video for *The Man*?

11. On the *ME!* music video, what is the last line Brendan Urie says in French, which is also the title of the next album single?

12. How many color-themed rooms were there in the *Lover* music video?

13. Which Taylor Swift song inspired the *Lover* music video to be set in a snow globe?

14. Who is the actor that voices the male version of Taylor Swift on the music video for *The Man*?

15. Who cameoed as the tennis umpire on *The Man* music video?

Answers on page 73

'Folklore' Album

1. How many tracks does *folklore* include?

2. On the song *betty*, Taylor Swift used the names of Blake Lively and Ryan Reynold's daughters in the lyrics. What were the two names?

3. When was *folklore* released?

4. What is the title of the bonus track from the *folklore* album?

5. How many songs did The National's Aaron Dessner co-write and produce in the *folklore* album?

6. Taylor Swift has mentioned that, in the *folklore* album, there are three songs that have themes of a "Teenage Love Triangle." Two are *august* and *betty* - what is the third?

7. Who was the "maddest woman this town has ever seen" Taylor Swift referenced in the song *the last great american dynasty*?

8. In the song *the last great american dynasty*, what was the name of the house in Rhode Island?

9. Who co-wrote the songs *betty* and *exile* alongside Taylor Swift?

10. Which song did Taylor Swift write by herself?

11. What was the first song that was written on the *folklore* album?

12. What did Taylor Swift name the stripped-down version of her folklore single *cardigan*?

13. What was the last song written for the album?

14. Which song was partially inspired by Taylor Swift's soldier grandfather?

15. What is the instrument Taylor Swift plays in the *cardigan* music video?

Answers on page 74

Romantic Relationships

1. Which boyband member broke up with Taylor Swift over the phone when she was 18?

2. Which Taylor Swift song was written about that boyband member?

3. How long was the infamous break-up phone call Taylor Swift received in 2008?

4. How long did Taylor Swift and Jake Gyllenhaal date?

5. Who was interviewing Taylor Swift when she revealed that she and Joe Jonas broke up?

6. How old was Taylor Swift when she dated John Mayer?

7. Who was the Scottish DJ and music producer Taylor Swift dated?

8. What was the pseudonym Taylor Swift used when she co-wrote a hit single with that DJ?

9. Who was the other half of the pairing nicknamed "Haylor"?

10. Who did Taylor Swift date from the famous Kennedy family?

11. Who wore an 'I heart T.S.' shirt at Taylor Swift's Independence Day party in 2016?

12. Who did Taylor Swift date from the cast of *The Twilight Saga* movies?

13. Which Taylor Swift song was written about that *Twilight* actor?

14. Which ex-boyfriend was *Dear John* about?

15. What is the name of the guy with whom Taylor Swift shared her first kiss?

Answers on page 75

Friends and Feuds

1. In 2019, who bought Taylor Swift's musical back catalogue for $300 million?

2. Who wrote a song featuring the line "I feel like me and Taylor might still have sex. Why? I made that b*tch famous"?

3. Who was Taylor Swift's high school best friend?

4. Which actress/model made Taylor Swift the godmother of her son?

5. What was the award show at which Kanye West interrupted Taylor Swift's acceptance speech?

6. Whose "one of the best videos of all time" did Kanye West vouch for when he interrupted that Taylor acceptance speech back in 2009?

7. Which female comedian apologized to Taylor after making a body-shaming joke at her expense on Instagram?

8. Who recorded and released the private conversation Taylor Swift had with Kanye West in 2016?

9. Which one of her friends has Taylor Swift appeared on a Vogue cover with?

10. Which Taylor Swift song was written about the relationship of her friends Lena Dunham and Jack Antonoff?

11. Who introduced Taylor Swift to her best friend Karlie Kloss?

12. With whom did Taylor Swift become best friends with when they were both dating members of the same band?

13. Who was the critic that attacked Taylor Swift's performance at her 52nd Grammy Performance, resulting in her writing a song about him?

14. With which musician did Taylor take a cooking class?

15. Which singer did Taylor Swift meet at the 2014 MTV Video Music Awards and later become close friends with?

Answers on page 76

Movie and TV Appearances

1. What is the name of Taylor Swift's 2020 documentary that was released on Netflix?

2. In which movie did Taylor Swift and Taylor Lautner play a couple?

3. Which animated movie did Taylor Swift and Zac Efron star in?

4. In what city was the 2019 City of Lover concert filmed?

5. What is Taylor Swift's one line of dialogue in the movie *Cats*?

6. Which song did Taylor Swift sing with the Jonas Brothers in the concert film *Jonas Brothers: The 3D Concert Experience*?

7. In the movie *Valentine's Day*, what did Taylor Swift receive as a gift from her boyfriend?

8. In which show did Taylor Swift make her TV acting debut?

9. What is the name of Taylor Swift's character in *Cats*?

10. In which Miley Cyrus film did Taylor cameo?

11. What song did Taylor Swift perform during her cameo in that Miley movie?

12. In which film did Taylor Swift star as Rosemary?

13. What is the title of the song Taylor Swift performs in the movie *Cats*?

14. What is the name of Taylor Swift's tree-loving character in the movie *The Lorax*?

15. In which TV show did Taylor Swift guest-star as Elaine, the long-time love of Shivrang?

Answers on page 77

Movie and TV Soundtracks

1. What was the name of the song Taylor Swift released for the soundtrack of *Fifty Shades Darker*?

2. What is the song Taylor Swift and Andrew Lloyd Webber wrote for the movie *Cats?*

3. To which movie soundtrack did Taylor Swift contribute the song *Today Was A Fairytale*?

4. For which movie did Taylor Swift write the song *You'll Always Find Your Way Back Home*?

5. To which movie soundtrack did Taylor Swift contribute the song *Safe & Sound*?

6. When Taylor Swift appeared on the TV show *CSI* in 2009, which song of hers did she remix for the show?

7. Which Taylor Swift song was debuted on the premiere of the fifth season of the show *Grey's Anatomy*?

8. Which song did Taylor write for the soundtrack of the film *One Chance*?

9. Which Taylor Swift movie song won a Grammy Award for Best Song Written for Visual Media?

10. Who was the *Cats* character that performed the song Taylor Swift wrote for the movie?

11. Which song from *The Hunger Games* soundtrack did Taylor Swift write about keeping a watchful eye in the Capitol?

12. What was the title of the music video in which Taylor walks through a cemetery in a white dress, then stumbles upon a Mockingjay pin?

13. Which song from a movie did Taylor Swift write two years before it was part of the movie's soundtrack?

14. Which Taylor song appears on both the *Valentine's Day* soundtrack and the platinum edition of *Fearless* album?

15. Which Taylor Swift movie song was made because Simon Cowell personally approached her for the project?

Answers on page 78

Music Videos

1. On the *You Need To Calm Down* music video, which drag queen impersonated Taylor Swift?

2. Which music video marked Taylor Swift's official solo directorial debut?

3. Which music video was dedicated to the petition to support the Equality Act?

4. Which music video was filmed in a dollhouse?

5. Which music video featured Taylor Swift as a cyborg?

6. Which Taylor Swift music video was the first to be shot and released during the COVID-19 pandemic?

7. Which Taylor Swift music video was filmed in near-total silence?

8. In which music video did Taylor Swift become invisible?

9. Which music video was based on Romeo and Juliet?

10. What was the first music video Taylor co-directed, with Roman White?

11. Which Taylor music video takes places in one continuous shot?

12. What color was the prom dress Taylor wore in the *Our Song* video?

13. Which Taylor Swift music video was filmed by the Seine in Paris?

14. Where in California did Taylor Swift film the music video for *22*?

15. Which Taylor Swift music video was shot in Africa?

Answers on page 79

Collaborations

1. Which legendary songwriter worked with Taylor on *Bad Blood*, *22* and *All You Had To Do Was Stay*?

2. In which Taylor Swift song did The Chicks feature?

3. Which John Mayer song was Taylor Swift featured in?

4. Who did Taylor Swift collaborate with on the song *Two Is Better Than One*?

5. What song did Taylor Swift and The Civil Wars collaborate on?

6. Who was the artist Taylor Swift sang with on the song *Both of Us*?

7. What is the first song Ed Sheeran and Taylor Swift collaborated on?

8. Who did Taylor Swift collaborate with on the song *ME!*?

9. Which Taylor Swift song featured Kendrick Lamar?

10. Who did Taylor Swift sing with on their single for the movie soundtrack of *Fifty Shades Darker*?

11. What is the name of the song that featured Ed Sheeran and Future?

12. Who did Taylor Swift sing with on her song *Exile*?

13. To which musical duo did Taylor Swift give her song *Babe*?

14. What is the title of the song Taylor Swift wrote for the band Little Big Town?

15. Which Tim McGraw song featured Taylor Swift and Keith Urban?

Answers on page 80

Awards and Accolades

1. Which album earned Taylor Swift her first Grammy?

2. Which album made Taylor Swift the first solo female artist to win a Grammy Award for Album of the Year twice?

3. Which album earned Taylor a nomination for Best New Artist at the 50th Grammy Awards?

4. How many Grammy Awards did *Speak Now* win?

5. Which song from *Speak Now* took home a Grammy?

6. Which Taylor Swift song has been certified diamond (having gone 10x platinum) by the RIAA?

7. In 2009, which Taylor music video won Best Female Video at the MTV Video Music Awards?

8. In 2012, which Taylor Swift song earned the 'Fastest Selling Single in Digital History' Guinness World Record?

9. In 2018, Taylor Swift became the most awarded female winner in AMA history with 23 awards. Which artist previously held the record?

10. Which magazine named Taylor Swift 'Icon of American Style' in 2011?

11. At which awards show did Taylor become the first woman to earn the title Artist of the Decade (the 2010s)?

12. At what age did Taylor Swift become the youngest artist to win a Grammy Award for Album of the Year?

13. What was the second music video Taylor Swift won Best Female Video for at the 2013 MTV Video Music Awards?

14. Which Taylor Swift record became the first album to win the American Music Country Award, Country Music Association, Academy of Country Music Award, and Grammy Award for Album of the Year?

15. Which award did Taylor Swift receive at Billboard's Women in Music ceremony?

Answers on page 81

Award Shows

1. What song did Taylor Swift perform during the 2012 American Music Awards?

2. At the 52nd Grammy Awards, Taylor Swift performed alongside who?

3. Also at the 52nd Grammy Awards, Taylor Swift performed the song *You Belong With Me* and which Fleetwood Mac song?

4. Which song did Taylor Swift perform with Miley Cyrus at the 51st Grammy Awards?

5. At the 2009 Academy of Country Music Awards, who was the magician Taylor Swift assisted to appear onstage?

6. Who presented Taylor Swift with the Kids' Choice Big Help Award in 2012?

7. Which song did Taylor Swift perform at the 54th Grammy Awards in which she changed the first line of the chorus to "Someday, I'll be singin' this at the Grammys"?

8. At which film festival did the documentary for the documentary *Taylor Swift: Miss Americana* premiere?

9. At which awards show did Taylor sit next to her boyfriend Joe Alwyn for the first time?

10. Considered as her first awards show performance since her three-year hiatus, what is the title of the song Taylor Swift performed at the 2018 American Music Awards?

11. At which awards show did Taylor Swift make the speech saying that there will be people who will try to "take credit for your fame"?

12. With which actor did Taylor co-host the 2016 Met Gala?

13. At which awards show did Taylor Swift present Kanye West with the Video Vanguard Award?

14. Which song did Taylor Swift perform at the 2014 MTV Video Music Awards, where the performance was 1920s-themed?

15. Which emotional song did Taylor Swift perform at the 2014 Grammy Awards where she whips her hair as she plays the piano?

Answers on page 82

Tours, Concerts, and Shows

1. Which tour did Taylor Swift first release a live album of?

2. What country was the first stop for the Asian leg of Taylor Swift's first world tour?

3. What was Taylor Swift's first all-stadium tour?

4. What was the name of Taylor Swift's first concert tour?

5. On her Netflix concert film, which two artists does Taylor Swift perform with during the song *Shake It Off*?

6. What is the title of Taylor Swift's sixth concert tour and first music festival tour?

7. How many songs from the *Taylor Swift* album did Taylor perform on her first headlining tour of *Fearless*?

8. On which Taylor Swift tour did Selena Gomez perform *Who Says* with Taylor at the Madison Square Garden?

9. Which song is the opening track to the *Red Tour*?

10. At which concert did Taylor Swift and Ed Sheeran first perform the song *End Game* live?

11. What was the first song Taylor sang at the 2014 Victoria's Secret Fashion Show?

12. During her *Reputation Tour*, what song did Taylor Swift perform the day before Mother's Day as a surprise song in 2018?

13. Which tour was postponed and rescheduled to 2021 due to the Coronavirus pandemic?

14. On the Netflix tour movie *Taylor Swift's Reputation Stadium Tour*, what was the surprise song in the concert?

15. On the first night of Taylor Swift's *Reputation Tour* in London, who was the special guest Taylor brought out and sang *Slow Hands* with?

Answers on page 83

Fandom

1. What is the name of the social networking app that Taylor Swift launched for her fans?

2. In what country did Lego display a mosaic portrait of Taylor Swift constructed from 35,840 Lego bricks?

3. What was the opening track to the *1989 World Tour*?

4. During her *Fearless Tour* and *Speak Now Tour*, what name was given to the room in which Taylor Swift and her band hung out, and where her mom would bring in fans from the crowd to meet Taylor Swift backstage?

5. Before the release of *1989*, how many fans did Taylor Swift invite to her house to listen to the album?

6. What does Taylor Swift call the meetings where she handpicks fans from social media and invites them to her house to listen to the album ahead of its release?

7. Which track number did fans notice Taylor reserves for her most vulnerable song on each album?

8. What was the title of the novel Taylor Swift wrote at 14?

9. What is the name of the parody music video Taylor Swift did with T-Pain that aired at the 2009 CMT Awards?

10. What is the rapper name of Taylor Swift that appeared on the parody rap music video she did with T-Pain?

11. During Taylor Swift's *1989* and *Reputation* tours in the US, what accessory was given to fans that lit up and changed color in time with the music?

12. What is the name Taylor Swift's band came up with while filming for the music video of *Picture to Burn*?

13. Which Taylor Swift song was released alongside her Netflix documentary *Miss Americana*?

14. What is the name given to the event where Taylor Swift handpicks fans from social media and gives them personalized Christmas presents?

15. What is the name of the first perfume Taylor launched?

Answers on page 84

Pets

1. Taylor named her cat after which character from the TV show *Law & Order: SVU*?

2. What is the name of the cat that Taylor Swift adopted on the set of the *ME!* music video?

3. Which music show judge did Taylor Swift's cats hang out with before the 2019 Billboard Music Awards in Las Vegas?

4. Which of Taylor Swift's cats had its face on Taylor's wristwatch in the music video for *You Need to Calm Down*?

5. Which cat is Taylor Swift holding in the *Blank Space* music video?

6. What is the title of the show starring Ellen Pompeo, after whose character Taylor Swift named one of her cats?

7. In which year did Taylor Swift get her first Scottish Fold cat?

8. Which of Taylor's cats appeared on a Diet Coke commercial with her?

9. What kind of cat did Taylor Swift adopt on the set of the *ME!* music video?

10. How did the cat handler describe the cat (that Taylor subsequently adopted) when it kept purring on her?

11. Which of Taylor Swift's cats was named after a character from a Brad Pitt movie?

12. What is the name of Taylor's mother's dog, a Great Dane who appears in *Miss Americana*?

13. Which of Taylor Swift's cats is the logo for her production company?

14. What trademark term did Taylor apply for on her cats' behalf?

15. What is the nickname for Taylor Swift's second Scottish-fold cat?

Answers on page 85

Anagrams

Can you unscramble these Taylor Swift song titles?

1. Raceway Tag?

2. A Woodenly Document?

3. Overtly So?

4. Anthem?

5. Hoofed Out Swot?

6. Goo Runs?

7. Loony Bond?

8. Banal Speck?

9. Dawdlers Items?

10. A Monkey Fright?

11. Acid Rang?

12. Fake to Fish?

13. Sooty Surf?

14. You Elbowing Them?

15. Buttercup Iron?

Answers on page 86

Complete the Lyric

Can you fill in the blanks in these Taylor lyrics?

1. "Oh my God, look at that face. You look like my next

_____." – *Blank Space*.

2. "Say you'll remember me, standing in a nice dress, staring

at the _____, babe." – *Wildest Dreams*.

3. "I go on too many dates, but I can't make 'em _____." –

Shake It Off.

4. "September saw a month of _____." – *Tim McGraw*.

5. "You made a _____ of a careless man's careful daughter."

– *Mine*.

6. "You're a redneck _____." – *Picture To Burn*.

7. "Loving him is like driving a new _____ down a dead-end

street." – *Red*.

8. "I was riding _____ with my hair undone in the front seat

of his car." – *Our Song*.

9. "The shape of your body, it's _____." – *Cruel Summer*.

10. "The ties were black, the _____ were white." – *Getaway Car*.

11. "It feels like a perfect night for breakfast at _____." – *22*.

12. "I can make the bad guys good for a _____." – *Blank Space*.

13. "You are somebody that I don't know, but you're takin' shots at me like it's _____." – *You Need To Calm Down*.

14. "Follow procedure, remember? Oh, wait, you got _____." – *Bad Blood*.

15. "And you know I love _____, faded blue jeans, Tennessee whiskey." – *London Boy*.

Answers on page 87

ANSWERS

Answers: General Knowledge

1. December 13, 1989.

2. Sagittarius.

3. 13.

4. Taylor Swift Productions. Nice and to-the-point!

5. Republic Records.

6. "Swifties".

7. Big Machine Records.

8. Scott Borchetta.

9. Blue.

10. 2019.

11. Abigail.

12. Alison.

13. 2014.

14. *New Year's Day*.

15. Sea urchins.

Answers: Songs

1. *22.*

2. *Dear John,* at 6 minutes, 43 seconds.

3. *Tim McGraw.*

4. *Soon You'll Get Better.*

5. *Hey Stephen.*

6. *Mine.*

7. *Welcome To New York.*

8. *Getaway Car.*

9. *Christmas Tree Farm.*

10. *Only The Young.*

11. *The Archer.*

12. *Death By A Thousand Cuts.*

13. *Invisible String.*

14. *Ronan.*

15. *Our Song.*

Answers: Early Life

1. *Kiss Me* by Sixpence None the Richer.

2. Pennsylvania.

3. He was a stockbroker.

4. Singer-songwriter James Taylor.

5. Austin.

6. A computer repairman.

7. *Lucky You*.

8. 14 years old.

9. Andrea and Scott.

10. Hendersonville High School.

11. Opera singer.

12. Philadelphia 76ers.

13. Faith Hill.

14. The Bluebird Café.

15. Robert.

Answers: Albums

1. *Lover.*

2. *Red.*

3. *reputation.*

4. *reputation.*

5. 'Daylight'.

6. *reputation.*

7. *folklore.*

8. *1989.*

9. 16 years old.

10. *Red.*

11. *Fearless.*

12. *Fearless.*

13. 6.

14. *Red.*

15. *1989.*

Answers: 'Taylor Swift' Album

1. *Teardrops On My Guitar.*

2. *Can't Tell Me Nothin'.*

3. Johnny.

4. Drew (Hardwick).

5. Jordan Alford.

6. *Cold As You.*

7. *Should've Said No.*

8. *Tied Together With A Smile.*

9. *Mary's Song (Oh My My My).*

10. Tim McGraw.

11. Liz Rose.

12. "Date nice boys."

13. *Should've Said No.*

14. *Picture To Burn.*

15. *Our Song.*

Answers: 'Fearless' Album

1. *Hey Stephen.*

2. *You Belong with Me.*

3. *The Best Day.*

4. *Jump Then Fall.*

5. 13.

6. *Change.*

7. Cheer captain.

8. Lucas Till.

9. 20 minutes.

10. *Love Story.*

11. "Junior Jewels".

12. *You Belong with Me.*

13. *White Horse.*

14. *Love Story.*

15. Colbie Caillat.

Answers: 'Speak Now' Album

1. 20 years old.

2. *Never Grow Up.*

3. *Innocent.*

4. *Sparks Fly.*

5. *Mine.*

6. *Story Of Us.*

7. Waiter.

8. *Story of Us.*

9. "TAY."

10. September.

11. *Mean.*

12. Joey King.

13. *Mine.*

14. *Back To December.*

15. *Story Of Us.*

Answers: 'Red' Album

1. *Begin Again.*

2. Nine.

3. *22.*

4. Wednesday.

5. *State of Grace.*

6. *We Are Never Ever Getting Back Together.*

7. *Begin Again.*

8. *I Knew You Were Trouble.*

9. Gary Lightbody.

10. Dark gray.

11. *22.*

12. *Red.*

13. *All Too Well*, at 5 minutes, 29 seconds.

14. Pink.

15. *Begin Again.*

Answers: '1989' Album

1. 20.

2. Wolves.

3. Scott Eastwood.

4. Ballet.

5. 36.

6. *Blank Space.*

7. Sean O'Pry.

8. "We never go out of style."

9. *Wildest Dreams.*

10. Catastrophe.

11. Selena Gomez.

12. 17.

13. *Bad Blood.*

14. Marjorie Finn.

15. "She lost him."

Answers: 'Reputation' Album

1. 13.

2. *Look What You Made Me Do.*

3. Whiskey on ice.

4. Joseph.

5. *...Ready for It?*

6. *Look What You Made Me Do.*

7. Snake.

8. *End Game* - featuring Future and Ed Sheeran.

9. *I'm Too Sexy* by Right Said Fred.

10. Arya Stark.

11. Tokyo.

12. *...Ready for It?*

13. Elizabeth Taylor.

14. Snake.

15. *New Year's Day.*

Answers: 'Lover' Album

1. Blake Lively and Ryan Reynolds.

2. *I Forgot That You Existed.*

3. A snake and butterflies.

4. *The Archer.*

5. January.

6. *Soon You'll Get Better.*

7. Saint-Tropez.

8. Katy Perry.

9. Butterfly.

10. Tyler Swift.

11. "You need to calm down."

12. Seven.

13. *You Are in Love.*

14. The Rock/Dwayne Johnson.

15. Scott Swift, aka Taylor Swift's father!

Answers: 'Folklore' Album

1. 16.

2. James and Inez.

3. July 24, 2020.

4. *the lakes*.

5. 11.

6. *cardigan*.

7. Rebekah Harkness.

8. Holiday House.

9. William Bowery.

10. *my tears ricochet*.

11. *my tears ricochet*.

12. *cabin in the candlelight*.

13. *hoax*.

14. *epiphany*.

15. Piano.

Answers: Romantic Relationships

1. Joe Jonas.

2. *Forever And Always.*

3. 27 seconds.

4. Three months.

5. Ellen DeGeneres.

6. 19 years old.

7. Calvin Harris.

8. Nils Sjöberg.

9. Harry Styles.

10. Conor Kennedy.

11. Tom Hiddleston.

12. Taylor Lautner.

13. *Back to December.*

14. John Mayer.

15. Drew.

Answers: Friends and Feuds

1. Scooter Braun.

2. Kanye West.

3. Abigail Anderson.

4. Jaime King.

5. MTV Video Music Awards.

6. Beyonce.

7. Nikki Glaser.

8. Kim Kardashian.

9. Karlie Kloss.

10. *You Are In Love.*

11. Lily Aldridge.

12. Selena Gomez.

13. Bob Lefsetz.

14. Lorde.

15. Camila Cabello.

Answers: Movie and TV Appearances

1. *Miss Americana.*

2. *Valentine's Day.*

3. *The Lorax.*

4. Paris.

5. "He's got soul!"

6. *Should've Said No.*

7. A giant teddy bear.

8. *CSI: Crime Scene Investigation.*

9. Bombalurina.

10. *Hannah Montana: The Movie.*

11. *Crazier.*

12. *The Giver.*

13. *Macavity The Mystery Cat.*

14. Audrey.

15. *New Girl.*

Answers: Movie and TV Soundtracks

1. *I Don't Wanna Live Forever.*

2. *Beautiful Ghosts.*

3. *Valentine's Day.*

4. *Hannah Montana: The Movie.*

5. *The Hunger Games.*

6. *You're Not Sorry.*

7. *White Horse.*

8. *Sweeter Than Fiction.*

9. *Safe & Sound.*

10. Victoria.

11. *Eyes Open.*

12. *Safe & Sound.*

13. *Today Was A Fairytale.*

14. *Jump Then Fall.*

15. *Sweeter Than Fiction.*

Answers: Music Videos

1. Jade Jolie.

2. *The Man.*

3. *You Need to Calm Down.*

4. *Lover.*

5. *...Ready for It?*

6. *cardigan.*

7. *You Need To Calm Down.*

8. *Delicate.*

9. *Love Story.*

10. *Mine.*

11. *We Are Never Ever Getting Back Together.*

12. Blue.

13. *Begin Again.*

14. Malibu.

15. *Wildest Dreams.*

Answers: Collaborations

1. Max Martin.

2. *Soon You'll Get Better.*

3. *Half of My Heart.*

4. Boys Like Girls.

5. *Safe & Sound.*

6. B.o.B.

7. *Everything Has Changed.*

8. Brendan Urie.

9. *Bad Blood.*

10. Zayn Malik.

11. *End Game.*

12. Bon Iver.

13. Sugarland.

14. *Better Man.*

15. *Highway Don't Care.*

Answers: Awards and Accolades

1. *Fearless.*

2. *1989.*

3. *Taylor Swift.*

4. Two.

5. *Mean.*

6. *Shake It Off.*

7. *You Belong with Me.*

8. *We Are Never Ever Getting Back Together.*

9. Whitney Houston.

10. Vogue.

11. American Music Awards.

12. 20 years old.

13. *I Knew You Were Trouble.*

14. *Fearless.*

15. Woman of the Decade.

Answers: Award Shows

1. *I Knew You Were Trouble.*

2. Stevie Nicks.

3. *Rhiannon.*

4. *Fifteen.*

5. David Copperfield.

6. Michelle Obama.

7. *Mean.*

8. The 2020 Sundance Film Festival.

9. 2020 Golden Globes.

10. *I Did Something Bad.*

11. The 2016 Grammy Awards.

12. Idris Elba.

13. 2015 VMA Awards.

14. *Shake It Off.*

15. *All Too Well.*

Answers: Tours, Concerts, and Shows

1. *Speak Now World Tour.*

2. Singapore.

3. *Reputation Stadium Tour.*

4. *Fearless Tour.*

5. Charli XCX and Camila Cabello.

6. *Lover Fest.*

7. Six.

8. *Speak Now Tour.*

9. *State of Grace.*

10. KIIS Jingle Ball concert.

11. *Blank Space.*

12. *The Best Day.*

13. *Lover Fest.*

14. *All Too Well.*

15. Niall Horan.

Answers: Fandom

1. The Swift App.

2. The UK.

3. *Welcome to New York.*

4. T-Party Room.

5. 89.

6. Secret Sessions.

7. Track 5.

8. *A Girl Named Girl.*

9. *Thug Story.*

10. T-Swizzle.

11. Wristbands.

12. The Agency.

13. *Only The Young.*

14. Swiftmas.

15. Wonderstruck.

Answers: Pets

1. Olivia Benson.

2. Benjamin Button.

3. Paula Abdul.

4. Benjamin Button.

5. Olivia Benson.

6. *Grey's Anatomy*.

7. 2011.

8. Olivia Benson.

9. Ragdoll kitten.

10. Purr box.

11. Benjamin Button.

12. Kitty.

13. Olivia Benson.

14. "Meredith Grey, Olivia Benson, and Benjamin Swift."

15. Dibbles.

Answers: Anagrams

1. Raceway Tag = *Getaway Car*.

2. A Woodenly Document = *You Need To Calm Down*.

3. Overtly So = *Love Story*.

4. Anthem = *The Man*.

5. Hoofed Out Swot = *Out Of The Woods*.

6. Goo Runs = *Our Song*.

7. Loony Bond = *London Boy*.

8. Banal Speck = *Blank Space*.

9. Dawdlers Items = *Wildest Dreams*.

10. A Monkey Fright = *King Of My Heart*.

11. Acid Rang = *Cardigan*.

12. Fake to Fish = *Shake It Off*.

13. Sooty Surf = *Story Of Us*.

14. You Elbowing Them = *You Belong With Me*.

15. Buttercup Iron = *Picture To Burn*.

Answers: Complete the Lyric

1. "Mistake".

2. "Sunset".

3. "Stay".

4. "Tears".

5. "Rebel".

6. "Heartbreak".

7. "Maserati".

8. "Shotgun".

9. "Blue".

10. "Lies".

11. "Midnight".

12. "Weekend".

13. "Patrón".

14. "Amnesia".

15. "Springsteen".

If you've enjoyed the book, please leave a review on Amazon: it only takes a minute and it really helps me to continue doing this! Take care - Alex.

Printed in Great Britain
by Amazon

73059359R00057